Little ECO EXPERTS

Ways to Take Care of the Planet

How to be guardians of the planet

PowerKiDS press

Published in 2023 by PowerKids, an Imprint of Rosen Publishing
29 East 21st Street, New York, NY 10010

Copyright © 2020 Editorial Sol90, S.L. Barcelona
All rights reserved.

No part of this book may be reproduced in any form without permission in writing from the publisher, except by a reviewer.

Cataloging-in-Publication Data
Names: Editorial Sol 90 (Firm).
Title: Ways to take care of the planet / by the editors at Sol90.
Description: New York : Powerkids Press, 2023. Series: Little eco experts
Includes glossary and index.
Identifiers: ISBN 9781725336964 (pbk.) ISBN 9781725336988 (library bound) ISBN 9781725336971 (6pack) ISBN 9781725336995 (ebook)
Subjects: LCSH: Environmental protection--Citizen participation--Juvenile literature. Environmental responsibility--Juvenile literature. Environmentalism--Juvenile literature.
Classification: LCC GE195.5 W397 2023 DDC 333.72--dc23

Coordination: Nuria Cicero
Editor: Alberto Hernández
Editor, Spanish: Diana Osorio
Layout: Àngels Rambla
Design Adaptation: Raúl Rodriguez, R studio T, NYC
Project Team: Vicente Ponce, Rosa Salvía, Paola Fornasaro
Scientific Advisory Services: Teresa Martínez Barchino

Imaging and infographics: www.infographics90.com
Firms: Getty/Thinkstock, AGE Fotostock, Cordon Press/Corbis, Shutterstock.

Manufactured in the United States of America

CPSIA Compliance Information: Batch #CSPK23. For Further Information contact Rosen Publishing, New York, New York at 1-800-237-9932.

CONTENTS

A Blue and Living Planet 4
The Diversity of Ecosystems. 6
A Land to Take Care Of 10
Dangers That We Must Prevent. 12
Lungs in Danger 14
What Are We Putting at Risk? 16
Poison in the Water 18
Earth Is Alive 22
Stormy Activity 24
What Can You Do?. 26
Steps in Favor of the Planet 30
Sick Coral 32
How Do Coral Reefs Get Sick?. 34
Freezing and Erosion 36
Glossary and Index 40

A BLUE AND LIVING PLANET

Earth is known as the "Blue Planet" because of the color of its oceans. These oceans cover two thirds of its crust. In addition, it is the only one of the planets that has liquid water on its surface.

Earth is not too close nor too far from the sun. That's why temperatures are mild and they render life as we know it.

The green areas of Earth are forests and jungles. These are vital ecosystems for the regeneration of oxygen.

The atmosphere allows the sun's solar radiation to enter—it is necessary for plants to grow. The atmosphere also regulates some harmful solar radiation by absorbing or reflecting the rays.

And, very importantly, the atmosphere is made of oxygen and carbon dioxide, essential gasses for life like humans.

THE DIVERSITY OF ECOSYSTEMS

Inside the landscapes that make up Earth, there are different ecosystems. These are biological systems where animals and plants live together. Ecosystems can be terrestrial or aquatic. Both can benefit human beings.

Square miles per ecosystem

1.5 million
(3.9 million square km)

2.7 million
(7 million square km)

3.8 million
(10 million square km)

Important Polar Regions
Polar sea ice helps regulate, or balance, the climate of the whole Earth!

6.6 million
(17 million square km)

8.8 million
(23 million square km)

Oceans and Valleys

Oceans are the greatest storehouse of carbon dioxide for the planet. As they are in contact with the lower portion of the atmosphere, they absorb a great portion of man-made CO_2 emissions. Oceans are also home to millions of species. In valleys, there are agricultural lands that enable the circulation of nutrients in the soil.

Square miles per ecosystem

| **135 million** | **232 million** | **16 million** |
| (439 million square km) | (600 million square km) | (41 million square km) |

DID YOU KNOW?

Our planet is unique. There is not another one like it where we could "move" to. That is why we must take care of it and preserve it for the benefit of future generations.

Oceans absorb a large part of the CO2 that humans emit.

14 million
(36 million square km)

13.5 million square miles
(35 million square km)

The **2** main classes of ecosystems: aquatic and terrestrial.

A LAND TO TAKE CARE OF

Earth is like a living organism that is in constant transformation and evolution.
In order to keep it healthy, we must take care of it, control all the threats that endanger it, and we must also preserve all the beings that inhabit it.

DANGERS THAT WE MUST PREVENT

Climate Change Worsening

One of the biggest challenges is to prevent climate change from intensifying, as its negative effects cause temperature changes and natural disasters. How? An important step towards achieving this goal is by reducing greenhouse gas emissions.

Not Limiting Greenhouse Gas emissions

Damaging Habitats

Cities must grow in a sustainable way by taking care of nature in order to prevent natural habitats from disappearing.

Hurting Wildlife

Uncontrolled hunting and fishing affect the animal populations; it may upset the healthy balance of ecosystems and lead to the disappearance of species.

Hurting wildlife

Damaging habitats

LUNGS IN DANGER

Despite efforts to raise public awareness and stop its destruction, one fifth of the Amazon rain forest has already disappeared. If no action is taken, almost half of the forest could disappear within two decades.

From a Forest to a Field

Fires are set to clear out land and use it for cattle grazing and agriculture.

Greenhouse Effect

By destroying vegetation, millions of tons of carbon that were fixed in plants are converted into carbon dioxide. This CO_2 ends up in the atmosphere and exacerbates the greenhouse effect.

AMAZON

Human Settlement

Industrial development attracts people to settle down in the region with little respect for nature.

Illegal mining

Aside from preparing land for cultivation, unspoiled areas in the Amazon have been deforested due to the illegal search for gold.

WHAT ARE WE PUTTING AT RISK?

Wildlife Diversity

There are 350 species of mammals, 1,000 bird species, 550 reptile species, and millons of insect species that live in the Amazon.

Birds
1,000
Species

Mammals
350
Species

Fish
3,000
Species

Reptiles
550
Species

Insects
10 mill.
Species

Plant Diversity

More than 10% of known worldwide plant species live in the Amazon.

Culture

Around 2.7 million Indigenous Peoples who live in the Amazon, from 350 different ethnic groups, are in danger of losing their cultural legacy, including 200 different languages.

20% of the Earth's oxygen is produced by the vegetation of the Amazon. That is why it is called the "lungs" of Earth.

POISON IN THE WATER

Eutrophication
This is a phenomenon that occurs due to an excess of nutrient substances (generally from human activities) in an aquatic ecosystem, such as a lake. This generates bacterias and some algae that consume oxygen from the water, which forces species to abandon their habitat.

Earth's aquatic ecosystems are suffering from invisible forms of pollution. Eutrophication and acidification of water destroys the diversity of aquatic life.

Acidification

The ocean absorbs 25% of CO_2 emissions. This high percentage acidifies the ocean water, damaging phytoplankton, corals, the shell of molluscs, and crustaceans.

THREATS

Pollution is the primary cause of eutrophication. Due to their high content of nitrogen, chemicals, urban waste, atmospheric precipitation, and agricultural operations produce nutrients that lead to eutrophic rivers, lakes, and estuaries. This harms the development of life in these aquatic ecosystems.

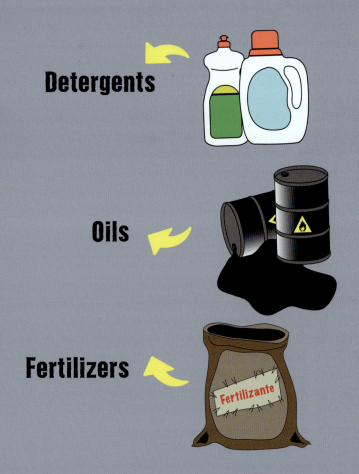

Detergents

Oils

Fertilizers

DID YOU KNOW?

Corals, starfish, and mussels, among other species, are like little architects; they use carbonates dissolved in water to build their shells and carapaces. However, the acidification of water dissolves these shells and carapaces.

EARTH IS ALIVE

Earth is not a dead rock. Unlike other planets, it enjoys life on its surface. And its interior is also active. Some of its activities may be destructive while others may be creative. Let's discover some of them.

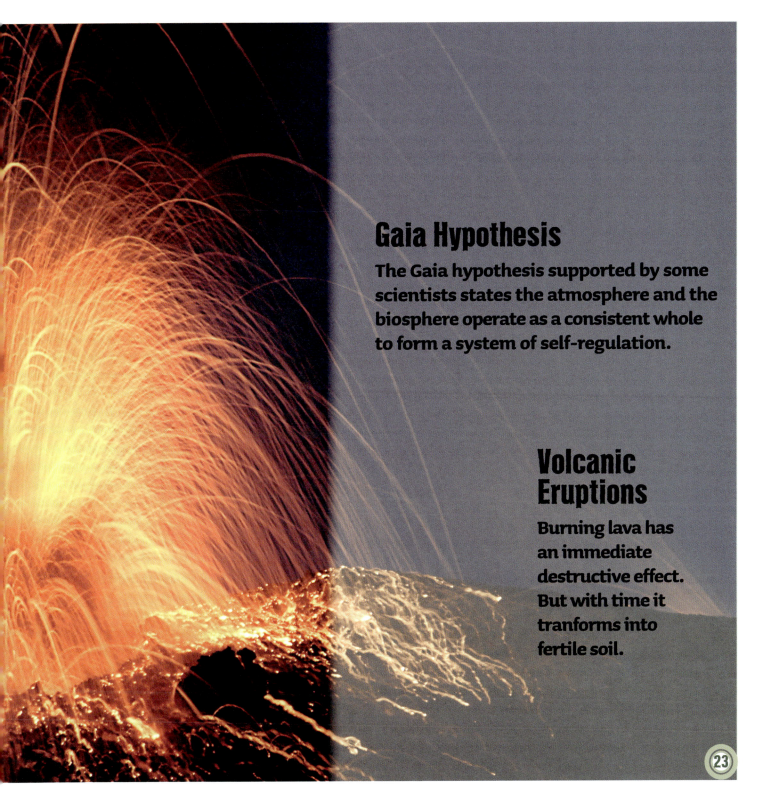

Gaia Hypothesis

The Gaia hypothesis supported by some scientists states the atmosphere and the biosphere operate as a consistent whole to form a system of self-regulation.

Volcanic Eruptions

Burning lava has an immediate destructive effect. But with time it tranforms into fertile soil.

STORMY ACTIVITY

Floods

The overflowing of rivers causes floods. But when these are cyclic, such as the Nile in Africa, they serve to fertilize fields.

Fires

It is a catastrophe when forests are set on fire. But in certain regions of the world, fires have beneficial effects.

Monsoon

This is a seasonal wind, loaded with heavy rain, that mainly falls in Southern Asia and in the Indian Ocean. These winds cause flooding, but they are essential to grow rich harvests.

WHAT CAN YOU DO?

Many people participate in organizations that devote themselves to protect the environment voluntarily. You can be an eco-volunteer! Here are **5** TASKS you can easily complete:

1 Clean Coasts and Beaches

Volunteers remove tons of plastic from beaches. Did know that plastic bags and other plastic products can kill fish, turtles, birds, and marine mammals?

2 Remove Invasive Plants

In some places, there are non-native plants that invade and alter ecosystems. This is the case of the Arundo donax in Mexico.

3 Plant Trees and Plants

Trees collect CO_2 and release oxygen, hold the ground together, fertilize soil, and shelter many species and animals. Planting trees gives life.

4 Build and Install Nest Boxes

Thanks to these simple boxes, birds can make their nests in forests with trees harmed by fires and other issues.

5 Report What Is Wrong

Impunity emboldens new aggressions against the environment. Report threats to the authorities or appropriate institutions in your country.

STEPS IN FAVOR OF THE PLANET

1 Reduce Waste
Select products without packaging.

2 Separate Garbage
Place each type of trash, such as foods that can be composted and cans that can be recycled, in the correct bin.

9 Respect Culture
We all have something to contribute.

8 Resepct Nature
Take care of plants and animals.

7 Save Energy
Turn lights off; fill up the washing machine.

3 Use Green Transport
Bike or use public transportation.

4 Consume Responsibly
Select organic products

5 Save Water
Do not waste it and use it imaginatively.

6 Use Renewable Energy
Select solar and wind energy.

SICK CORAL

Coral reefs protect the coasts from erosion, provide economic support to millions of people, and are home to 25% of fish species worldwide. But one third of the world's reefs are sick because of climate change and human activity.

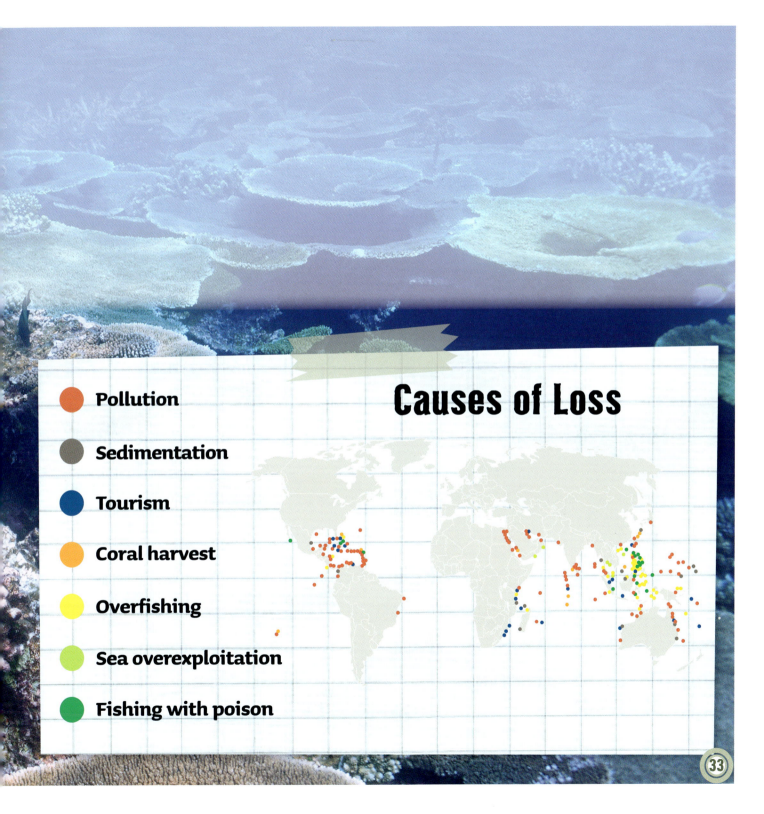

HOW DO CORAL REEFS GET SICK?

When the average water temperature rises, the zooxanthellae algae leave coral polyps, which, lacking food, become ill, turn white, and die.

Healthy Coral

Polyps

Corals are big structures formed by millions of polyps, microscopic animals which are related to jellyfish and anemomes.

Polyp

Algae

Symbiosis

Zooxanthellae algae live inside polyps and provide food for them. In return, polyps offer shelter and protection for algae.

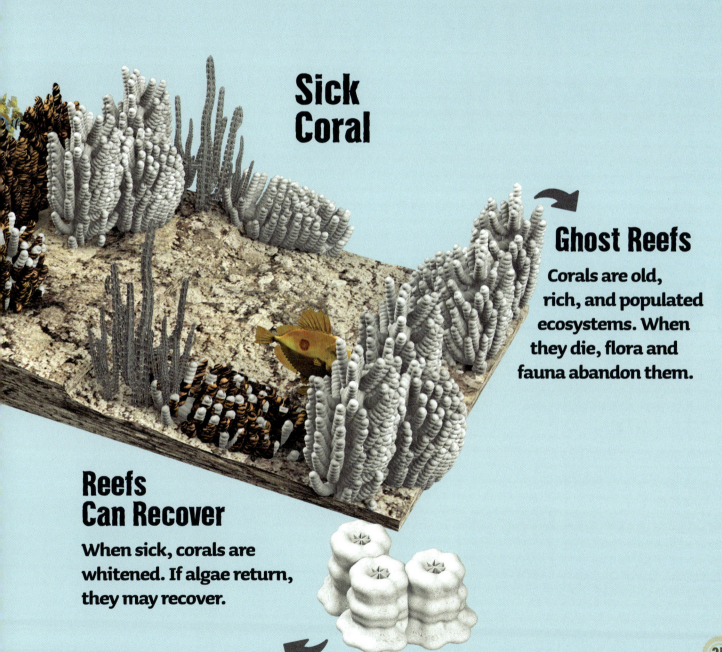

Sick Coral

Ghost Reefs
Corals are old, rich, and populated ecosystems. When they die, flora and fauna abandon them.

Reefs Can Recover
When sick, corals are whitened. If algae return, they may recover.

FREEZING AND EROSION

Through this experiment, you will understand the transformation of the landscape throughout different glacial and interglacial periods, such as an ice age. The main thing you need is a regular rock!

YOU WILL NEED:
- 1 medium-sized rock
- 1 plastic cup
- 1 plastic bag
- Water and paper
- 1 freezer

STEP BY STEP: find the instructions on the next page!

STEP ONE

Place the rock inside the cup and fill it up with water. Leave it out all night so that it may become damp.

STEP TWO

Remove the rock from the cup and place it in a plastic bag. Then place the rock in the cup and leave it in the freezer for 2 hours.

STEP THREE

Remove the rock from the freezer and wait for it to unfreeze, and until the ice melts and reaches room temperature.

STEP FOUR

Place a white piece of paper on top of the table. Open the bag and drop the rock on top of the paper while you watch from a safe distance. You will see how pieces of rock will detach themselves.

Conclusion

Water will infiltrate through tiny cracks in the rock. Once the water freezes, it will expand with so much strength that it fragments the rock.

Glossary

algae: Plantlike living things that are mostly found in water.

architect: A person who designs buildings.

atmosphere: The mixture of gases that surround a planet.

carbon dioxide (CO_2): A gas breathed out by animals.

desertification: The system by which an area becomes a desert.

erosion: The act of wearing away by water, wind, or ice.

habitat: The natural place where an animal or plant lives.

impunity: Being free from punishment, harm, or loss.

radiation: Waves of energy.

Index

Amazon, 14, 15, 16, 17

chemicals, 20

cities, 12

climate change, 12, 32

experiment, 36

farming (agriculture), 11, 14

fires, 14, 24, 29

Gaia hypothesis, 23

ocean, 4, 8, 9, 19, 24

oxygen, 4, 5, 17, 18, 28

sun, 4, 5

plants, 5, 6, 14, 28, 30

plastic, 26

trees, 28, 29

volunteer, 26

wildlife, 13, 16